MICHEL ROUX

sauces for sweets

Dedication
To my son Alain, who cooks side-by-side with me at The Waterside Inn.

Contents

4	Foreword
6	About Sauces
8	**Recipes**
10	Syrup and Fruit Coulis
22	Sweet Sauces
32	Custard Sauces
36	Sabayons
40	Creams
50	Chocolate Sauces
52	Ice Creams
58	Sorbets
63	Index

Foreword

When I think about the recipes in this book—fruit coulis full of natural goodness, dessert sauces so delicious that they can be eaten alone with a spoon, refreshing ice creams and sorbets, elegant creams and *sabayons* to accompany desserts and gâteaux—my face breaks into an enormous, sweet, sugary smile.

Without even closing my eyes, I can remember myself at five years old, picking blackberries, standing on tiptoe, lost among the tangle of brambles. As soon as we returned home, I would seize the *mouli* and push through the blackberries to make the sweetest-smelling purée. My mother would add a spoonful of sugar and the juice of a lemon to transform it into a coulis, then she would make us a rice pudding topped with caramel, which we ate the moment it had cooled, surrounded by a sea of the black-currant coulis. Words cannot describe our greedy pleasure.

If greed is a deadly sin, then I have been committing one since my childhood and I am happy to continue doing so, because I adore being a gourmand. That memory of blackberry picking also reminds me of gathering fallen pears from under the tree at Charolles. Maman would carefully poach the ripest fruit in a little water and sugar. Then she reduced the cooking liquid to make a light syrup to glaze the cherry tarts or *clafoutis*, which were our Sunday treat. She never needed to bid me to come to the table; I would be seated the moment the tart came out of the oven, waiting patiently for the divine moment …. My tastebuds were enflamed by the waves of sugary sweetness wafting out of the tart, and my mouth started to water.

Later, at the age of fourteen, I began my apprenticeship to a *pâtissier*—a fairytale existence. The realm of mousses and creams, which my mother had never explored, was now revealed to me.

Top of my hit parade was Chiboust Cream, which I adored for its lightness, its velvety consistency, and the ease with which I could pipe it with a plain or fluted tip. During my apprenticeship, I also discovered "couverture," the wonderful chocolate used by *pâtissiers* for Easter eggs and chocolate animals, and also for sauces. I learned that a few mint leaves infused in milk add a special freshness to these chocolate sauces and help to develop the flavor. More recently, I have taken to using basil instead of peppery mint. It adds a new dimension to the sauce.

To my mind, all the sweet sauces, coulis, ice creams, and sorbets jostle for popularity. I adore them all and indulge my creativity and my mood, inventing variations or entirely new versions, always taking care not to compromise the flavor of the main ingredient.

All fruits are marvelous, bursting with vitamins essential to our wellbeing. I can only encourage every one of you, young and old, to eat them in abundance. There are so many varieties of every fruit (about 1500 types of pears, for example). Presented with such a vast array, the uninformed shopper finds it hard to know which to choose. Truly food for thought for those *pâtissiers* who have a notion to create a recipe for every single one!

About Sauces

From time immemorial, children have been attracted to the sweet scents of vanilla, lemon, and sugar, which their mothers and grandmothers used in preparing desserts. Once, the creams and sauces that accompanied these sweet treats were laden with butter, cream, and eggs, but nowadays the fashion is for healthier, lighter sauces, which are every bit as delicious as the old classics. Today, fruit sauces and coulis are used to accompany and enhance all kinds of desserts, from charlottes, mousses, and cakes to warm fruit tarts, while fruit sorbets add a magical, refreshing note to the end of a meal.

The golden rules

The vital ground rules for following a recipe to make a successful sauce are:

- Have ready to hand all the equipment you will need for the recipe.
- Measure all the ingredients before embarking on the recipe.
- Remember that the preparation time given for the recipes begins after all the ingredients have been measured and all the equipment is ready.

The Basic Ingredients

To achieve a perfect result when making sauces, creams, and ices, you must make sure that your basic ingredients, like butter, eggs, and cream, are ultra-fresh and of the finest quality.

Butter: Unless otherwise specified, always use the best unsalted butter.

Chocolate: Use only top-quality chocolate to make your sauces. For the best results, serve chocolate sauces at the correct temperature of 85–105°F.

Eggs: I use large eggs, weighing 2–2½ ounces. Some recipes use only egg yolks or whites. To save waste, freeze any surplus; egg whites can be frozen just as they are and will keep well for up to six months. Yolks should be lightly beaten with 5–10 percent of their weight of sugar before freezing. Do not keep them for more than four weeks. Defrost both whites and yolks before using.

Gelatin: I use leaf gelatin, sold in 1-ounce packages of about 8 leaves. If these are hard to find, substitute a ¼-ounce envelope of powdered gelatin for every 4–5 leaves and dissolve it in a little warm water before using.

Flour: This should always be all-purpose flour, sifted before using.

Sweet Sauces

Choose the sauce for a dessert according to the main ingredient. The purpose of a dessert sauce is to accompany the principal ingredient, but never to dominate it. Remember that the dessert comes at the end of a meal; being the last dish, it creates the final and lasting impression, so it must be perfect.

Creams

With their varied colors and textures, creams are velvety and delicately flavored. By judiciously mixing different creams, you can come up with some surprising and delectable results, with unusual colors and flavors. Be careful, though; practise on your family first and never experiment if you are expecting guests!

Creams do not keep well; they can be stored in the refrigerator for no more than two or three days. Take them out of the refrigerator for about 30 minutes before using. Very few creams can be successfully frozen.

Fruit coulis

These deliciously refreshing sauces, with their bright glowing colors and flavors, range from sweet to bitter or acid, depending on the fruit used. They can be enhanced with a touch of spice, but take care not to overpower the intrinsic flavor of the fruit.

All fruit coulis can be kept in an airtight container in the refrigerator for several days.

Ice creams and sorbets

Of all desserts, these get everyone's vote. All ice creams and sorbets are divine, whether they are based on milk, eggs, cream, or fruit, or are absolutely plain or flavored with alcohol or spices. It is as easy to whip up an ice as it is to mix a cocktail. Domestic ice cream makers are simple to use and are becoming cheaper and more efficient all the time. The recipes in this book are intended only for home consumption, not for commercial use, so they contain no stabilizing or preserving ingredients or other additives, which do nothing for the flavor of the ice cream anyway.

Ices can provide an environment in which harmful organisms could thrive. To avoid this danger, heat the mixture to 175°F for 15 seconds before cooling and churning, and make sure that all your equipment is scrupulously clean.

Recipes

Poached pears with
Blackberry Coulis (page 12)

- The star of sweet sauces is *crème anglaise*, the famous classic and well-loved sweet custard, which is sadly often one of the most ill-used and badly made. *Crème anglaise* should be creamy, unctuous, rich yet delicate, with a superb mouth feel. When it is like this, I adore it, supping it up with a spoon like soup. But when it is watery, insipid, and depressingly unsatisfying on the palate, I can hardly swallow it. This is why I have made my recipe as explicit as possible, and illustrated it with clear step-by-step instructions.
- Fruit coulis add a refreshing tang to desserts and fresh fruits. They should be served directly on the plate with the dessert arranged on top, or trickled around the edge in a ribbon, but never poured over the dessert, which would spoil its appearance.
- Never serve more than two coulis on the same plate. Each coulis has its own distinctive flavor which could be diametrically opposed to another. To maintain the harmony, avoid the temptation to combine a riot of different colors on the plate.
- Many dessert sauces are delicious with ice creams and sorbets. What could be more divine than vanilla or cinnamon ice cream coated with warm chocolate sauce? Naturally, homemade ices taste infinitely better than any you can buy. To enjoy them at their best, eat them when they are freshly churned.

Stock Syrup

This basic syrup is used with fresh fruits to make fruit sorbets and coulis that can accompany any number of desserts.

Ingredients:
2 cups sugar
1½ cups cold water

Makes about 3 cups
Preparation time: **5 minutes**
Cooking time: **about 7 minutes**

Combine the sugar and water in a saucepan and bring slowly to a boil over low heat, stirring continuously with a wooden spoon. Boil for 3 minutes, skimming the surface if necessary. Pass the syrup through a wire-mesh conical sieve and leave to cool before refrigerating. The syrup will keep in an airtight container in the refrigerator for up to 2 weeks.

Grapefruit Coulis with Mint

This refreshing coulis marries well with orange desserts, chocolate charlotte, or black-currant sorbet. It looks very attractive if you scatter on a few mint leaves, snipped as finely as possible, just before serving.

Ingredients:
2 grapefruit, preferably pink, each about 1 pound
¼ cup fresh mint, snipped
3½ tablespoons sugar
⅔ cup plain yogurt
5 teaspoons vodka

Serves 6
Preparation time: **5 minutes**

Using a knife with a flexible blade, peel the grapefruit, removing all pith and membrane, and cut each one into six. Place in a blender with the mint and sugar, whizz for 1 minute, and pass through a wire-mesh conical sieve into a mixing bowl. Whisk in the yogurt, then mix in the vodka. Serve very cold.

Red-Currant Coulis

This is the simplest fruit sauce or coulis imaginable, but the simplest is often the best. With no cooking, the freshness of the fruit is preserved and the sauce tastes sublime. It is perfect served with white-fleshed fruits such as peaches and pears, or with vanilla ice cream and iced soufflés.

Ingredients:

2¼ cups red currrants, stripped off the stem
Juice of 1 lemon
½ cup Sorbet Syrup (opposite)

Serves 4
Preparation time: **3 minutes**

Put all the ingredients in a blender and whizz for 30 seconds. Strain through a conical strainer and *voilà* — the sauce is ready to use. It will keep for up to 3 days in the refrigerator.

Black-Currant Coulis

This fresh-tasting black-currant sauce makes an unusual accompaniment to Floating Islands (picture, page 18). You can use thawed frozen black currants instead of fresh if you prefer.

Ingredients:

3 cups fresh black currants, stems removed
⅔ cup Sorbet Syrup (opposite)
Juice of 1 lemon
Sugar

Serves 6
Preparation time: **5 minutes**

Thoroughly rinse and drain the black currants. Place in a blender with the syrup and lemon juice, and process until smooth. Strain through a nylon sieve (metal will discolor and taint the black currants) into a bowl. Taste the coulis and add extra sugar if necessary. Cover and chill in the refrigerator until needed.

Strawberry Coulis with Green Peppercorns

I usually serve this coulis poured around a lemon sorbet, vanilla ice cream, or perhaps a poached pear or pear charlotte. Occasionally in summer I make amuse-gueules *of thinly sliced marinated raw tuna encircled by a ribbon of this refreshing sauce.*

Ingredients:

1½ pints very ripe strawberries, hulled
1½ tablespoons soft green bottled peppercorns, well drained
½ cup Stock Syrup (page 10)
Juice of ½ lemon
1 tablespoon poppy seeds (optional)

Serves 8

Preparation time: **5 minutes**

Put the strawberries, peppercorns, syrup, and lemon juice in a blender (1) and whizz for 1 minute to make a purée (2 and 3). Pass the coulis through a wire-mesh conical sieve into a bowl (4) and, if you wish, add the poppy seeds just before serving.

Blackberry Coulis

This divine coulis can accompany almost all charlottes, whatever their flavor. It is equally delicious served with poached pears (picture, page 8), parfaits or iced bombes, or ice creams such as coconut, vanilla, or banana.

Ingredients:

2½ cups ripe blackberries, hulled
¼ cup kirsch
⅔ cup Stock Syrup (page 10)
Juice of ½ lemon

Serves 8

Preparation time: **5 minutes**

Put all the ingredients in a blender and whizz for about 1 minute, until puréed. Rub the sauce through a wire-mesh conical sieve and serve cold.

Coulis of Pears with Red Wine

Serve this powerful and delicious coulis with an iced vacherin, a Saint-Honoré *filled with whipped cream with an accompaniment of red berries, or with a simple compote of fresh apricots.*

Ingredients:

3 very ripe pears, each about 7 ounces
A pinch of ground cinnamon
½ cup red wine, preferably Bordeaux
2 tablespoons cold water
Juice of ½ lemon
¾ cup sugar

Serves 6

Preparation time: 10 minutes, plus 30 minutes' marinating

Peel and core the pears. Cut them into small pieces and place in a bowl with the cinnamon and red wine. Cover with plastic wrap and leave to marinate for 30 minutes.

Combine the water, lemon juice, and sugar in a thick-bottomed saucepan. Heat the mixture over very low heat and bubble it gently until it becomes a pale caramel. Take the pan off the heat and pour in the red wine in which you marinated the pears. (Be careful not to get splashed as the cold wine hits the hot caramel.) After 5 minutes, stir the diluted and cooled caramel with a wooden spoon, then pour it over the pears. Transfer to a blender and whizz for 1 minute, then chill the coulis before serving. If it becomes too thick, dilute it with 2 or 3 spoons of cold water.

Rhubarb Coulis

This refreshing sauce goes very well with a nougat glacé *or a meringue-based* vacherin, *which can be too rich and sugary on their own. Depending on the time of year and the age of the rhubarb, you may need to adjust the amount of water for the cooking.*

Ingredients:
8 ounces tender young rhubarb stems, cut in small cubes
½ cup water
½ cup sugar
1 vanilla bean, split lengthwise

Serves 6
Preparation time: **3 minutes**
Cooking time: **about 8 minutes**

Put all the ingredients in a saucepan and bring gently to a boil. As soon as the rhubarb is soft enough to crush with a spoon, stop cooking and remove the vanilla bean.

Put the rhubarb in a blender and purée for 2 minutes, then pass through a conical sieve. Keep the resulting coulis at room temperature to retain its delicate perfume. If it seems too thick, add a little cold water just before serving.

Red-Fruit Coulis

This fresh-tasting coulis makes the most of delicious summer fruits. Serve it with desserts based on red fruits such as strawberries and raspberries.

Ingredients:
1 cup strawberries
1 cup raspberries
3 tablespoons sugar
Juice of ½ lemon
2 tablespoons water

Serves 4
Preparation time: **5 minutes**

Wash, drain, and hull the strawberries. Hull the raspberries but do not wash them.

Put the fruit in a blender with the sugar, lemon juice, and water. Purée for 1 minute, then strain through a conical sieve and chill in the refrigerator before serving.

Grape Coulis with Armagnac

Make this delicious coulis in the fall, when a bunch of grapes is worth its weight in gold. I like to use muscat de Hambourg grapes, bursting with sweet juice and sunshine flavor, but these are only available in Europe, and then only from August until mid-September. On no account be tempted to use seedless grapes. They simply do not have enough flavor. This coulis is wonderful served with lady fingers, and it enhances the flavor of fresh sun-ripened figs like a dream.

   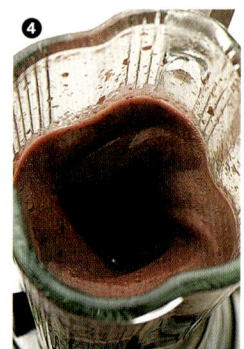

Ingredients:
4 tablespoons butter
⅓ cup sugar
2–3 cups red grapes, seeded
⅓ cup Armagnac

Serves 6
Preparation time: **5 minutes**
Cooking time: **about 20 minutes**

Melt the butter in a saucepan (1), stir in the sugar, and add the grapes. Cook gently over low heat for about 20 minutes (2), then pour in the Armagnac and ignite it (3). When the flames have died down, let the grapes cool in their syrup for a few minutes.

Put the contents of the pan in a blender and whizz for 30 seconds (4), then pass through a conical sieve. Keep the sauce in the refrigerator until ready to use and stir just before serving.

Mango Coulis with Saffron

I was thrilled with my idea of substituting this succulent coulis for Crème Anglaise (page 33) in a dish of floating islands (soft poached meringues on a sea of sauce). You could also serve this wonderful sauce with a "hedgehog" of mango slices stuck with toasted flaked almonds and a scattering of wild strawberries. The marriage of colors and flavors is divine.

Serves 6
Preparation time: 5 minutes

Ingredients:
1 cup mango flesh, diced
1 cup Stock Syrup (page 10)
Juice of ½ lemon
A pinch of saffron threads

Put the mango in a blender with the lemon juice and all but 2 tablespoons of the stock syrup. Purée the mixture for 2 minutes, then strain through a conical sieve.

Warm the reserved syrup with the saffron threads in a small saucepan, then let cool. When the syrup is cold, mix it into the mango coulis and refrigerate until ready to serve.

Floating Islands on a sea of Mango Coulis with Saffron

Coulis of Peaches with Scented Honey

A real discovery for those who have never tasted this sauce, which is superb served with slices of toasted brioche, or simply poured generously over a dish of wild strawberries.

Ingredients:

- 4 very ripe peaches, preferably white-fleshed
- Juice of 1 lemon
- 4 tablespoons honey, preferably flower-scented
- ⅔ cup water
- 1 sprig of flowering lavender (optional)

Serves 6

Preparation time: **6 minutes**

Cooking time: **about 8 minutes**

Peel the peaches, cut in half, and remove the pits. Put them in a saucepan with the lemon juice, honey, and water and bring to a boil over low heat. Poach gently for 5 minutes, then add the sprig of lavender, if using, and cook for 30 seconds longer.

Let cool for a few minutes, then transfer the contents of the pan to a blender and whizz for 1 minute. Pass the sauce through a conical sieve and let cool completely. When cold, refrigerate until ready to use.

White Peach Coulis with Star Anise

This coulis is the perfect accompaniment for white peaches, either raw or lightly poached in syrup and served cold or warm. It is also excellent with wild strawberries or any delicate fruits.

Ingredients:

2 very ripe white peaches
1¾ cups water
¾ cup sugar
4 star anise and 2 cloves, tied up together in a square of cheesecloth
Juice of 1 lemon
Juice of 2 oranges, preferably blood oranges
1 tablespoon grenadine syrup (if you are not using blood oranges)

Serves 8

Preparation time: **10 minutes**

Cooking time: **about 20 minutes**

Put the peaches in a bowl, cover with boiling water (1), and leave for 15 seconds, then transfer to a bowl of cold water, using a slotted spoon. Skin and halve them with a sharp knife, leaving in the pits.

Place the halved peaches with their pits in a small saucepan. Add the water, sugar, star anise, cloves, and lemon juice, set over low heat, and bring to just below boiling point. Simmer for 20 minutes (2), then let cool at room temperature for 15 minutes.

Discard the peach pits and spices. Purée the contents of the pan in a blender for about 2 minutes (3), to make a smooth coulis. Pass this through a fine-mesh conical sieve and keep in a cool place.

Strain the orange juice into a small saucepan. Add the grenadine and reduce the juice over low heat to make an orange syrup. Reserve it in a ramekin.

Pour the peach coulis around the fruits on individual plates and spoon a ribbon of orange syrup onto it. Using a toothpick or the tip of a knife, delicately swirl the orange syrup into the coulis.

❶

Hot Apricot Sauce

This sauce is excellent served with baked apples, exotic fruit soufflés, and ice creams made with nuts such as almonds and walnuts.

Ingredients:
- 10 ounces very ripe apricots
- ⅓ cup sugar
- Scant 1 cup water
- 1 tablespoon finely snipped mint leaves
- 1 tablespoon kirsch (optional)

Serves 6
Preparation time: **5 minutes**
Cooking time: **about 10 minutes**

Cut the apricots in half and remove the pits. Put the fruit in a saucepan with the sugar and water, and cook gently for about 10 minutes, until tender. The precise time will depend on the ripeness of the apricots. Transfer to a blender and purée for 1 minute, then pass the sauce through a conical strainer.

Add the mint and kirsch, if using. Serve the sauce hot so that it retains all its aroma.

Hot Caramel Butter Sauce

Serve this rich sauce with vanilla ice cream or a piping hot apple dessert like apple charlotte. Delicious!

Ingredients:
- 1 vanilla bean
- 1¾ cups light cream
- ½ cup Stock Syrup (page 10)
- ⅓ cup sugar
- 6 tablespoons unsalted or slightly salted butter, according to taste

Serves 8
Preparation time: **5 minutes**
Cooking time: **about 7 minutes**

Split the vanilla bean lengthwise and scrape out the inside with the tip of a knife. Place the seeds in a saucepan with the cream, syrup, and sugar. Heat and bubble gently, stirring continuously with a small whisk, until the mixture is the color of pale hazelnuts, then stir in the butter in small pieces until completely amalgamated and smooth. Serve the sauce very hot.

Mint Sauce

This creamy, refreshing sauce is excellent served with orange and grapefruit sections or a strawberry cake dessert such as gâteau fraisier, *or as a substitute for* Crème Anglaise *(page 33) to accompany Floating Islands.*

Ingredients:
1 cup milk
½ cup plus 2 tablespoons sugar
1 cup fresh mint
3 egg yolks
1 tablespoon snipped mint leaves
A few drops of green peppermint syrup

Serves 4
Preparation time: **15 minutes**
Cooking time: **about 5 minutes**

Put the milk and ½ cup of the sugar into a saucepan and bring slowly to a boil over low heat. As soon as it boils, remove from the heat, add the mint, cover, and leave to infuse for 10 minutes.

Put the egg yolks and remaining sugar in a bowl and whisk to a foamy ribbon consistency. Pour the milk infusion onto the egg mixture, stirring all the time. Return the mixture to the saucepan and cook gently over low heat, stirring continuously, until the temperature of the custard reaches about 175°F and it is thick enough to coat the back of a spoon. Run your finger down the spoon; it should leave a clear trail. Immediately pass the sauce through a wire-mesh conical sieve into a clean bowl. Leave to cool at room temperature, stirring occasionally to stop the sauce from coagulating and a skin from forming.

Cover the cold sauce with plastic wrap and refrigerate for up to 48 hours. Just before serving, add the snipped mint and a few drops of green mint syrup.

Rum Sauce

The perfect complement to bread pudding, Christmas plum pudding, and rum and raisin ice cream.

Ingredients:
1¼ cups heavy cream
5 tablespoons sugar
2 teaspoons cornstarch mixed with 2 tablespoons milk
⅓ cup dark rum
2 tablespoons golden raisins, blanched refreshed, and drained

Serves 6
Preparation time: **5 minutes**
Cooking time: **about 10 minutes**

Put the cream and sugar in a small saucepan and bring to a boil over low heat. Add the cornstarch, stirring as you go, bubble for 2 minutes, then pour in the rum. Simmer for 2 minutes longer, stir in the raisins, and serve piping hot.

Honey Sauce

This ambrosial sauce, lightly perfumed with honey, is delicious with pancakes, crisp apple tartlets, French toast, and ice cream.

Serves 8
Preparation time: **5 minutes**
Cooking time: **about 10 minutes**

Ingredients:
1⅓ cups ripe bananas
Juice of 1 lemon
1¼ cups Stock Syrup (page 10)
2 teaspoons ground ginger
3 tablespoons honey

Cut the bananas in slices and immediately toss them in the lemon juice (1). Put them in a saucepan with the syrup, ginger, and honey (2) and boil for 5 minutes. Purée in a blender for 1 minute, then pass the sauce through a wire-mesh conical sieve into a bowl (3). Stir until cold, cover with plastic wrap, and refrigerate until ready to use.

Red-Wine Sauce

I serve this sauce with poached peaches or pears, or to enhance the flavor and aroma of a molded rice pudding. You can also churn the sauce to make an excellent sorbet; just stir in 1/3 cup water before churning.

Serves 8
Preparation time: 5 minutes
Cooking time: about 10 minutes

Ingredients:

2 cups red wine
1 cinnamon stick, crushed
1 clove
2 vanilla beans, split lengthwise
Juice and zest of 1 orange
1 cup sugar
A small pinch of freshly grated nutmeg
1 tablespoon mint leaves

Put all the ingredients except the nutmeg and mint in a saucepan (1). Cook gently until the liquid has reduced by one-third (2). Remove from the heat, add the nutmeg and mint, then pass the sauce through a wire-mesh conical sieve (3).

Let cool completely, then refrigerate until ready to use.

Licorice Sauce

This unusual sauce has a delicious flavor of licorice, which perfectly complements a pear tart, plum clafoutis, pistachio ice cream, or a compote of yellow peaches. I add whipped cream just before serving to lighten and soften the sauce. Without the addition of the cream, it will keep well in the refrigerator for 48 hours, covered with plastic wrap.

Ingredients:
3 egg yolks
⅓ cup sugar
1 cup milk
2 ounces black licorice sticks, cut in small pieces
¼ cup heavy cream, whipped until floppy

Serves 6
Preparation time: 15 minutes
Cooking time: about 5 minutes

Follow the method for *Crème Anglaise* (page 33), substituting the licorice for the vanilla. Add the whipped cream just before serving.

Caramel Sauce

This simple, delicious sauce can be served with a multitude of desserts, and can even be stirred into plain yogurt. It will keep well in an airtight container in the refrigerator for several days.

Ingredients:
½ cup sugar
5 tablespoons butter, softened
1 vanilla bean, split lengthwise and seeds scraped out with the tip of a knife
2 cups heavy cream

Serves 6
Preparation time: 5 minutes
Cooking time: about 15 minutes

In a thick-bottomed saucepan, combine the sugar, butter, and the seeds from the vanilla bean. Set over very low heat and stir continuously with a wooden spoon until the sugar has dissolved completely. Continue to cook until the mixture turns an attractive caramel color. Immediately take the pan off the heat and stir in the cream, taking care that you are not spattered as the cold cream hits the hot caramel. Mix well and cook the sauce over medium heat for 5 minutes, stirring continuously with the wooden spoon. The sauce should be perfectly blended, pliable, and shiny. Pass it through a wire-mesh conical sieve and let cool at room temperature before serving.

Rich Caramel Sauce

This sauce should be served very cold. It can also be churned in an ice cream maker to make a splendid caramel ice cream. For a less rich sauce, you can omit the egg yolks, but they do make the sauce smoother, less liquid, and more refined.

Ingredients:
½ cup sugar
⅓ cup water
2 cups heavy cream
2 egg yolks, lightly beaten

Serves 6
Preparation time: **5 minutes**
Cooking time: **about 5 minutes**

Put the sugar and water in a large saucepan and cook over low heat until the sugar has completely dissolved and is coming to a boil. Wash down the inside of the pan with a pastry brush dipped in cold water to prevent any crystals from forming. Cook the sugar until it turns a lovely deep amber and the surface begins to smoke slightly. Immediately take the pan off the heat and beat in the cream, whisking continuously.

Return the pan to a high heat and stir the sauce with a whisk. Let the sauce bubble for 2–3 minutes, then take off the heat.

Still stirring, pour a little of the sauce onto the egg yolks. Pour the mixture back into the pan and heat very gently; on no account let it boil. Pass the sauce through a conical sieve into a bowl and leave in a cool place until cold. Stir it from time to time to prevent a skin from forming.

Banana Sauce

This simple sauce with a Caribbean flavor makes a perfect accompaniment to a dish of exotic fruits.

Ingredients:

2 medium bananas
Juice of 1 lemon
⅔ cup water
1¾ cups sugar
1 cup crème fraîche
½ cup white rum
⅔ cup milk

Serves 8
Preparation time: **10 minutes**
Cooking time: **about 20 minutes**

Peel the bananas, cut in rounds, and immediately mix with the lemon juice to stop them from turning brown.

Put the water and sugar in a saucepan and cook to a pale caramel. Remove from the heat, add all the other ingredients, and mix gently with a spatula. Return the pan to medium heat and cook at a gentle bubble for about 20 minutes, delicately stirring the mixture all the time.

Let the sauce cool slightly, then transfer to a blender and whizz for 1 minute. Pass the sauce through a conical strainer and keep it in the refrigerator until ready to use.

Autumnal Sauce

This autumnal sauce is lovely with a compote of peaches or figs, or with baked apples.

Ingredients:

1 apple, about 4 ounces
2 medium bananas
Juice of 1 lemon
2 heaping tablespoons honey
Seeds from 2 cardamom pods
½ cup sugar
1 cup water

Serves 8
Preparation time: **5 minutes**
Cooking time: **10 minutes**

Peel and core the apple and dice it finely. Peel the bananas and cut them in rounds.

Put the prepared fruits in a saucepan with the lemon juice, honey, cardamom seeds, sugar, and water, and bring to a boil over low heat. Simmer very gently for 10 minutes, then pour into a blender and purée for 1 minute, or until very smooth. Pass the sauce through a conical sieve into a bowl, leave at room temperature until cold, then refrigerate until ready to use.

Banana Sauce served with exotic fruits and strawberries

Prune and Armagnac Sauce

This sauce is ideal in the fall, served with molded rice pudding, a hot soufflé of marrons glacés, *pear or banana ice cream, and, of course, prune* clafoutis.

Ingredients:

½ pound prunes, preferably Agen, soaked in cold water for 6 hours

¾ cup sugar

½ cinnamon stick

⅔ cup Armagnac

1 cup butter

Serves 10

Preparation time: **10 minutes**

Cooking time: **about 30 minutes**

Drain the soaked prunes, place them in a saucepan with the sugar and cinnamon, and cover with cold water. Bring slowly to a boil over low heat and simmer for 20 minutes. Transfer to a bowl, remove the cinnamon, and leave the prunes to cool, then drain and pit them. Reserve the cooking syrup.

Cut six of the prunes into small, even pieces and reserve them in a bowl. Put the remaining prunes in a shallow pan with the Armagnac, ⅔ cup cooking syrup from the prunes, and 7 tablespoons butter. Heat gently without boiling to about 140–158°F. Transfer to a blender and whizz for 1 minute. Scrape the puréed prunes into a saucepan and whisk in the remaining butter, a small piece at a time, and enough of the reserved syrup to give the sauce a light ribbon consistency. Add the prune pieces and serve the sauce tepid, or keep it in a *bain-marie* filled with not-too-hot water for a maximum of 30 minutes.

Orange Butter Sauce

This is delicious served with crêpes, lemon charlotte, a warm plum tart, or a chocolate soufflé. A few drops of Grand Marnier or Curaçao add extra warmth to the sauce in winter.

Serves 6
Preparation time: 5 minutes
Cooking time: about 5 minutes

Ingredients:
Juice of 6 oranges, each about ½ pound, strained through a conical sieve
½ cup plus 6 tablespoons confectioners' sugar
9 tablespoons butter, softened to a paste

Put the orange juice and sugar in a saucepan and reduce by half over medium heat. Remove from the heat and whisk in the softened butter, a little at a time. Serve the sauce at room temperature.

Warm plum tart with Orange Butter Sauce

Crème Anglaise

Crème anglaise *(custard sauce)* can accompany any number of cold desserts. For a light, foamy, unctuous sauce to serve with a hot dessert like apple charlotte, warm rice pudding, or chocolate soufflé, warm the custard slightly and add a little Grand Marnier, champagne, or other alcohol, then whizz it in a blender for 30 seconds. Crème anglaise *can also be churned to make the ever-popular vanilla ice cream.*

Makes about 3 cups
Preparation time: 15 minutes
Cooking time: about 5 minutes

Ingredients:
6 egg yolks
½ cup plus 2 tablespoons sugar
2 cups milk
1 vanilla bean, split lengthwise

In a bowl, whisk the egg yolks with one-third of the sugar (1) until the mixture is pale and has a ribbon consistency (2). Put the milk, vanilla, and the remaining sugar in a saucepan, stir with a whisk for a few seconds (3), then bring to a boil. Pour the boiling milk onto the egg yolks, whisking continuously. Return the mixture to the pan and cook gently, stirring with a wooden spoon (4), until the temperature of the custard reaches about 175°F. It should have thickened enough to coat the back of the wooden spoon and for your finger to leave a trail when you run it down the spoon.

Remove the vanilla bean and immediately pour the sauce into a clean bowl set in crushed ice to speed up the cooling process. Stir the custard occasionally with a wooden spoon to stop it from coagulating and prevent a skin from forming. Once it is completely cold, cover with plastic wrap and refrigerate for a minimum of 2 and a maximum of 48 hours.

Coffee or Chocolate Crème Anglaise:

For a coffee or chocolate *crème anglaise*, replace the vanilla with 2 tablespoons instant coffee powder or 2 ounces melted bittersweet chocolate (5). Check the consistency of the sauce on the back of a wooden spoon (6).

Lemon Sauce

This sharp lemony sauce makes the perfect summer dessert with red fruits such as strawberries, raspberries, black currants, and red currants. To accentuate the flavor, sprinkle on some shreds of candied lemon zest just before serving. If the lemons are very tart, you may need to add more sugar to the juice.

Ingredients:
1 cup light cream
¾ cup sugar
1 cup lemon juice (from about 6 lemons)
6 egg yolks

Serves 4
Preparation time: **15 minutes**
Cooking time: **about 5 minutes**

Put the cream, ⅛ cup sugar, and the lemon juice in a saucepan, stir, and bring to a boil. Whisk the egg yolks with the remaining sugar in a bowl, to a ribbon consistency. Pour the boiling cream onto the egg mixture, whisking continuously. Pour the mixture back into the saucepan and cook very gently for 2 minutes, stirring continuously with a wooden spoon or spatula. On no account let it boil. Pass it through a conical sieve into a bowl and leave in a cool place, stirring occasionally to prevent a skin from forming. When the custard is cold, cover the bowl with plastic wrap and refrigerate.

Jasmine Tea Sauce

This delectable sauce is based on a recipe of the late, great chef Alain Chapel. It is especially delicious served with a slice of freshly broiled brioche, sprinkled with a veil of confectioners' sugar.

Ingredients:
8 egg yolks
¾ cup firmly packed brown sugar
½ cup milk
3 cups light cream
3 tablespoons jasmine tea leaves

Serves 4
Preparation time: **15 minutes**
Cooking time: **about 20 minutes, plus 30 minutes infusing**

Put the egg yolks and brown sugar in a bowl and work together lightly with a wooden spoon for about 1 minute.

Pour ⅛ cup milk and 1 cup cream into a small saucepan and bring to a boil. Immediately remove the pan from the heat and stir in the tea leaves. Cover the pan and leave to infuse for 2 minutes.

Pour the hot infusion onto the egg mixture and mix thoroughly. Stir in the remaining cream and leave to infuse at room temperature for 30 minutes.

Pass the mixture through a conical sieve into a clean saucepan and cook very gently for about 5 minutes, stirring continuously with a wooden spoon. Pour into a bowl and stir in the remaining milk. Let cool, stirring occasionally to prevent a skin from forming. Cover and chill until ready to serve.

Kirsch Sabayon

Many people are nervous about attempting to make a sabayon and fear that it will curdle. There is very little risk of this if you use a bain-marie or a heat diffuser.

When serving a sabayon as part of a dessert (like red fruits or raspberry-filled pancakes), spoon it over the dessert and place under a hot broiler until the top turns a light nutty brown.

Ingredients:

½ cup plus 1 tablespoon sugar
½ cup water
6 egg yolks
½ cup kirsch

Serves 4

Cooking time: **10–12 minutes, plus cooling**

Put the sugar and water in a small saucepan, bring to a boil, and let cool.

Add the egg yolks and ⅓ of the kirsch (1). If you are feeling very confident, pour the mixture into a saucepan, place the pan on a heat diffuser over very low heat, and whisk continuously until you have a smooth, rich mousse. Alternatively, set the bowl over a pan of simmering water, making sure that the bottom of the bowl is not in direct contact with the water. Whisk to obtain a rich, smooth mousse, then increase the heat and continue to whisk until the sabayon has a ribbon consistency (2). Stir in the remaining kirsch and remove the pan from the heat. Use the sabayon as soon as possible.

Summer fruits with glazed Kirsch Sabayon

Coffee Sabayon with Tia Maria

This sabayon *is really a dessert in itself, but it also makes a delicious sauce for such puddings as* gâteau de riz impératrice, apple tart, or pears poached in syrup.

Ingredients:
¼ cup cold water
2 tablespoons instant coffee
¼ cup sugar
4 egg yolks
¼ cup Tia Maria

Serves 4
Preparation time: *15–20 minutes*
Cooking time: *15–20 minutes*

Half-fill with warm water a saucepan large enough to hold the base of a mixing bowl. Combine the cold water and coffee in the bowl and whisk with a balloon whisk to dissolve the coffee. Still whisking, add all the other ingredients.

Stand the base of the bowl in the saucepan of water and set the pan over medium heat. Start whisking and continue to do so for 10–12 minutes. The temperature of the water in the saucepan must not exceed 195°F, or the *sabayon* will start to coagulate. It is ready when it reaches the consistency of egg whites beaten to soft peaks, with an unctuous, shiny, fluffy, and light texture and a temperature not exceeding 130°F. As soon as the *sabayon* is ready, stop whisking, spoon it into bowls, large glasses, or a sauceboat, and serve immediately.

Caramel Sabayon

Serve this simple and delicious sabayon *with any fruits of your choice macerated in white rum. Pour it over the fruit and place briefly under a hot broiler until the* sabayon *is just tinged with color.*

Ingredients:
½ cup sugar
½ cup heavy cream
4 egg yolks
Juice of 1 lemon

Special Equipment:
Candy thermometer

Serves 4

Cooking time: **about 10 minutes, plus cooling**

Heat the sugar in a medium, heavy saucepan, until it begins to liquefy and darken. Stir with a wooden spoon until the caramel is clear and the color of honey. Immediately remove the pan from the heat.

Take great care at this stage. Standing well back, add the cream to the caramel. It will spit and bubble vigorously for a few seconds. When the bubbling subsides, stir and reheat gently until the caramel has completely dissolved and the cream is smooth. Let cool completely.

Put the egg yolks in a clean saucepan and add the cooled caramel cream. Add the lemon juice, set over very low heat, and whisk well. Use a candy thermometer to test the temperature. As soon as the *sabayon* reaches 140°F, take the pan off the heat. If you don't have a candy thermometer, test the sauce with your finger. At the correct temperature, it will be too hot for your finger to bear more than the briefest dip. Use the *sabayon* immediately.

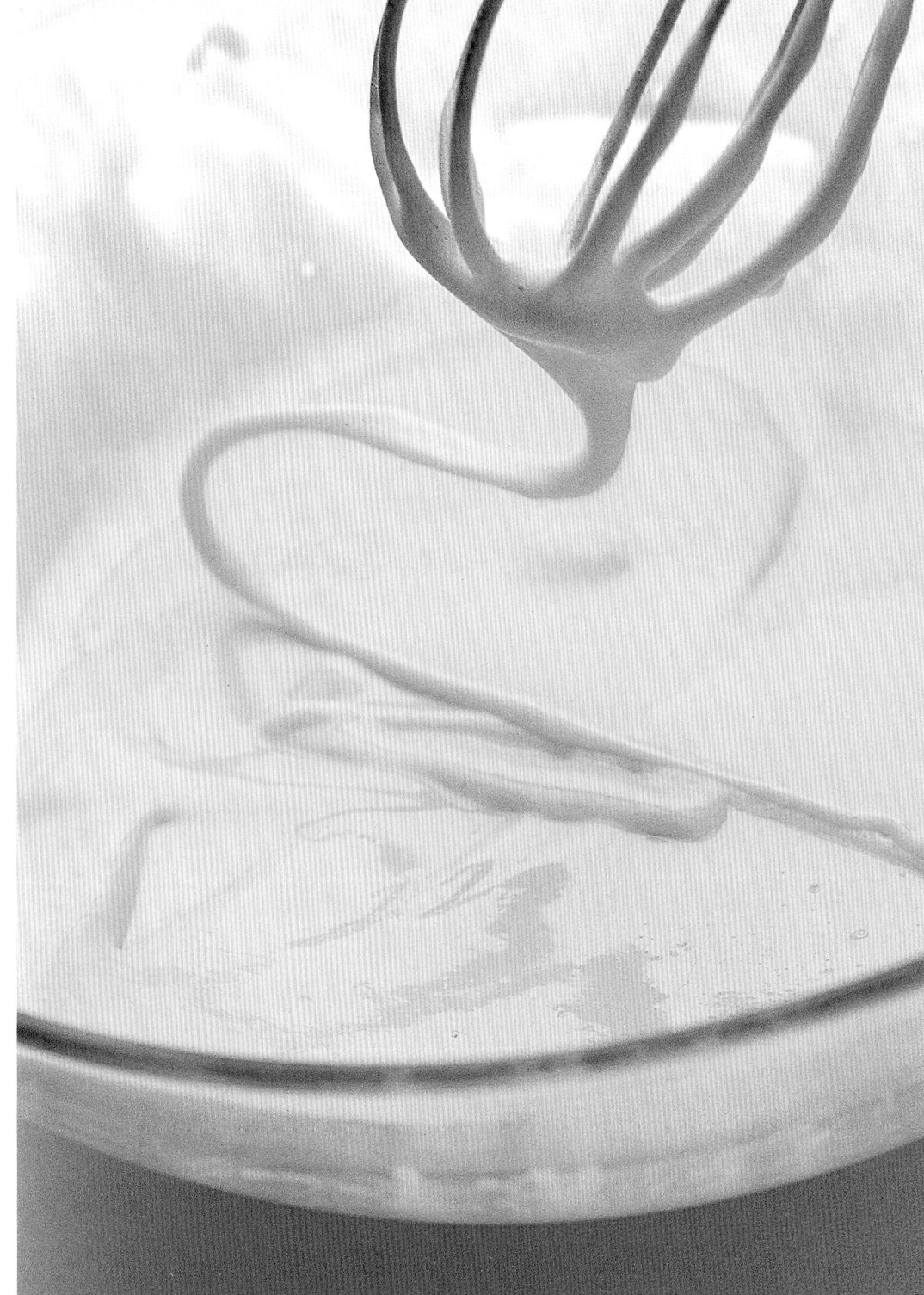

Pastry Cream

Pastry cream is to desserts what veal stock is to savory sauces—it forms the basis for innumerable recipes. It is as simple to make as it is delicious.

Makes about 3 cups
Preparation and cooking time: **15 minutes**

Ingredients:
6 egg yolks
⅔ cup sugar
½ cup all-purpose flour
2 cups milk
1 vanilla bean, split lengthwise
Butter or confectioners' sugar, for coating

Put the egg yolks and 3 tablespoons sugar in a bowl and whisk until thick and frothy. Sift in the flour and mix until smooth (1).

Mix the milk, the remaining sugar, and the vanilla bean in a saucepan and bring to a boil. Remove the vanilla bean and pour one-third of the boiling milk onto the egg mixture, whisking continuously (2). Pour this mixture back into the pan and gently bring back to a boil over low heat, stirring all the time (3). Simmer for 2 minutes until smooth and thickened, then pour into a bowl and let cool. Dot a little butter over the surface (4), dust with confectioners' sugar, or cover the bowl tightly with plastic wrap to prevent a skin from forming as the pastry cream cools.

Whisk the Pastry Cream until it is smooth and luscious

Chiboust Cream

This fragile but delectable cream is used in festive desserts like puits d'amour *(picture opposite). If you like, substitute Curaçao, Grand Marnier, or rum for the vanilla in the pastry cream.*

Ingredients:
1 recipe Pastry Cream (page 41), cooled to tepid, vanilla bean removed
1 recipe freshly-made Italian Meringue (page 44), cooled to tepid

Makes 5 cups
Preparation time: *25 minutes*

Remove the vanilla bean from the tepid pastry cream, then fold in one-third of the meringue, using a whisk. Use a spatula to fold in the rest of the meringue very delicately; if you overwork the mixture, it will collapse and lose its lightness.

For a more robust Chiboust Cream, make the pastry cream with a liqueur of your choice. Warm this gently, stir in 2 gelatin leaves or 1 tablespoon powdered gelatin, and dissolve, then fold into the pastry cream before cooling.

Chocolate Chiboust Cream: Add 3 ounces melted bittersweet chocolate to the pastry cream before cooling.

Chiboust Cream is used as a filling for puits d'amour *("wells of love")*

Italian Meringue

This cooked meringue is used to lighten various creams, like Buttercream (opposite) and Chiboust Cream (page 42). The quantities given here are the minimum needed to give a really good result, but you can keep any excess in an airtight container in the refrigerator for up to a week.

Ingredients:
6 egg whites
⅓ cup water
1¾ cups sugar

Special Equipment:
Candy thermometer

Makes about 3 cups
Preparation time: **7 minutes**
Cooking time: **15 minutes**

Put the egg whites in the bowl of an electric mixer. Mix the water and sugar in a heavy saucepan. Bring to a boil over medium heat, stirring with a skimmer. Skim the surface and brush down any sugar crystals that form on the inside of the pan, using a pastry brush dipped in cold water. Increase the heat so that the syrup boils rapidly and put in a candy thermometer to check the temperature.

When the temperature of the syrup reaches 230°F, beat the egg whites until well risen and stiff. Keep an eye on the syrup and take the pan off the heat as soon as it reaches 250°F.

With the mixer on the lowest speed, gently pour the syrup onto the beaten egg whites in a thin stream, taking care not to let it run onto the beaters. Continue beating at low speed for about 15 minutes, until the meringue is almost cold. It is now ready to use.

Buttercream

This simple cream is easy to make and is not too rich or sickly. It can be used in all sorts of cake-based desserts.

Ingredients:
1 recipe freshly-made Italian Meringue (opposite), cooled to tepid
32 tablespoons butter, at room temperature

Makes about 4 cups
Preparation time: **about 10 minutes**

Set the mixer containing the meringue on low speed and beat in the butter, a little at a time. Continue beating for about 5 minutes until the buttercream is very smooth and homogeneous. Use immediately, or put in an airtight container and keep in the refrigerator for up to a week. If you do this, leave the buttercream at room temperature for 1 hour before using, then mix well until very smooth.

Chantilly Cream

Chantilly Cream is used to lighten and enrich numerous desserts. It can also be served just as it is to complement all kinds of desserts, fruits, and ice creams. Chill the mixing bowl before making the cream.

Ingredients:
2 cups light cream, well chilled
½ cup confectioners' sugar, or ¼ cup Stock Syrup (page 10)
Vanilla powder or extract

Makes about 2 cups
Preparation time: **8 minutes**

Place the chilled cream, sugar, or syrup and vanilla to taste in the chilled bowl of an electric mixer and beat at medium speed for 1–2 minutes. Increase the speed and beat for 3–4 minutes, until the cream begins to thicken and the whisk leaves a thick ribbon trail when lifted. Do not overbeat, or the cream may turn into butter.

Chocolate Chantilly Cream: Add 2 tablespoons sifted unsweetened cocoa powder to the cream before whipping, or melt 6 ounces bittersweet chocolate and fold in one-third of the cream, then fold this mixture delicately into the remaining cream.

Coffee Chantilly Cream: Dissolve 2 tablespoons instant coffee (or 1 tablespoon coffee extract) in 1 tablespoon hot milk and add to the cream before whipping.

Praline Cream

The delicate, nutty flavor of this cream makes it perfect for filling all kinds of cake-based desserts.

Ingredients:

⅔ cup shelled hazelnuts
2 cups Pastry Cream (page 41)
1 recipe Chantilly Cream (page 45)
6 ounces praline or nougat paste
A pinch of confectioners' sugar

Makes 5 cups
Preparation time: 20 minutes

Heat the broiler to very hot. Spread the hazelnuts in the broiler pan and place under the hot broiler to detach the papery skins. Rub them in a dish towel (1) to remove the skins completely (2). Return the hazelnuts to the broiler pan, sprinkle with confectioners' sugar and broil until lightly caramelized (3). Let cool completely, then chop with a knife (4) or crush coarsely with a rolling pin.

Put one-third of the pastry cream in a bowl with the praline or nougat paste (5) and whisk until thoroughly mixed (6). Add the rest of the pastry cream and mix well again with the whisk.

Using a spatula, gently fold in the Chantilly Cream (7). Fold in the chopped hazelnuts just before using the praline cream (8).

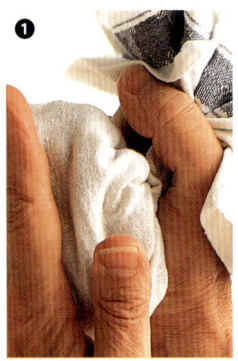

Frangipane

This delicious almond cream is used in several desserts, including a pithiviers. For a moister, smoother mixture, stir in 20–30 percent of pastry cream just before using.

Ingredients:

1⅔ cups blanched almonds, ground finely in a blender

2½ cups confectioners' sugar

16 tablespoons butter, at room temperature

⅓ cup all-purpose flour

5 eggs

¼ cup rum (optional)

Makes about 4 cups

Preparation time: **20 minutes**

Sift together the ground almonds and confectioners' sugar.

Put the butter in an electric mixer and beat until very soft. With the motor still running, beat in the ground almond and sugar mixture. When it is all incorporated, add the flour, then beat in the eggs, one at a time, beating well between each addition until the cream is light and homogeneous. Stir in the rum, if using.

Use the frangipane immediately, or cover with plastic wrap and keep in the refrigerator for up to 5 days. If you do this, leave it at room temperature for 30 minutes before using.

Mousseline Cream

This light, palatable cream is less rich than buttercream and makes a superb filling for tarts and tartlets. Use it as it is, or add any flavoring of your choice, such as caramel, chocolate, coffee, praline, or Grand Marnier.

Ingredients:

1 recipe Pastry Cream (page 41), freshly made using 4 whole eggs and 2 egg yolks

16 tablespoons butter, at room temperature

Flavoring of your choice (optional)

Makes about 5 cups

Preparation time: **30 minutes**

Cut one-third of the butter into small pieces. As soon as you have made the pastry cream, remove the pan from the heat and beat in the butter. Pour into a bowl and leave in a cool place, stirring from time to time to cool the mixture faster and prevent a skin from forming. Put the remaining butter in an electric mixer and beat at low speed for about 3 minutes, until fairly pale. Increase the speed to medium and add the cooled pastry cream, a little at a time. Beat for 5 minutes longer, until the cream is perfectly light and creamy. Leave it plain, or stir in the flavoring of your choice. Use immediately, or cover with plastic wrap and keep in the refrigerator for up to 4 days.

Chocolate Cream

This cream is very rich and velvety without being sickly. It is used in many cake-based desserts and in all sorts of chocolate confections.

Ingredients:
1 cup heavy cream
¾ cup sugar
1½ cups unsweetened cocoa powder, sifted, or bittersweet chocolate, chopped
12 tablespoons butter, at room temperature

Makes about 3 cups
Preparation time: **15 minutes**

Put the cream and sugar in a saucepan, place over high heat, and bring to a boil, stirring continuously. Boil for 3 minutes, then remove the pan from the heat and stir in the cocoa or chopped chocolate and half the butter, a little at a time. Pour the mixture into a bowl and leave in a cool place until completely cold. Stir from time to time to prevent a skin from forming.

Put the remaining butter in an electric mixer and beat for 3 minutes, or until very light and fluffy. Still beating, add the cold chocolate cream, a spoonful at a time, and beat until the mixture is completely amalgamated and very light in texture, almost like a mousse.

Use the chocolate cream immediately, or keep in an airtight container in the refrigerator for up to 3 days.

Rich Chocolate Sauce

This rich, velvety sauce is ideal spooned over vanilla or coffee ice cream or meringues filled with whipped cream. It evokes memories of childhood.

Ingredients:
7 ounces best-quality bittersweet chocolate or couverture, chopped
⅔ cup milk
2 tablespoons heavy cream
2½ tablespoons sugar
2 tablespoons butter, diced

Serves 6
Preparation time: **10 minutes**
Cooking time: **about 5 minutes**

Put the chocolate in a bowl and gently melt it over a pan of simmering water, stirring with a wooden spoon until very smooth. Combine the milk, cream, and sugar in a saucepan, stir with a whisk, and bring to a boil. Still stirring, pour the boiling milk mixture onto the melted chocolate, then return the mixture to the pan and bubble it for a few seconds, stirring continuously. Remove from the heat and add the butter, a little at a time, whisking until the sauce is smooth and homogeneous. Pass it through a wire-mesh conical sieve and serve hot.

Light Chocolate Sauce

This light sauce has a good bitter chocolate flavor. It is easy to prepare and is satisfyingly low in calories. Serve it in ladlefuls with profiteroles, ice creams, and pear desserts.

Ingredients:
1 cup plus 2 tablespoons unsweetened cocoa powder
¾ cup sugar
1½ cups water
1½ tablespoons butter, softened

Serves 6
Preparation time: **10 minutes**
Cooking time: **about 5 minutes**

Combine the cocoa, sugar, and water in a saucepan and whisk until well amalgamated. Bring to a boil over low heat, whisking continuously, and boil for 2 minutes. Whisk in the butter, a little at a time, and cook for 2 minutes longer. Serve the sauce immediately or keep it warm in a *bain-marie* for a few minutes.

Quick Chocolate Sauce

Perfect for impatient cooks, this sauce can be prepared in a trice. Children will adore it served with pancakes, waffles, or vanilla ice cream. To develop the chocolate flavor to the full, infuse some basil leaves in the cream.

Ingredients:
8 ounces bittersweet chocolate, chopped
1¼ cups light cream
1 tablespoon basil leaves (optional)

Serves 6
Preparation time: **5 minutes**
Cooking time: **3 minutes**

Heat the cream in a saucepan until just beginning to bubble, then add the chocolate, stirring with a whisk. Reduce the heat to low and cook gently until the sauce is smooth and creamy, then pour it into a bowl or sauceboat and serve immediately. If you are using basil leaves, add them to the cream before heating and strain the sauce through a conical sieve.

White Chocolate Sauce with Mint

The mint adds freshness to this sauce, which is delicious served over dark chocolate ice cream scattered with a few pistachios.

Ingredients:
8 ounces white couverture or best quality white chocolate, chopped
½ cup milk
1 cup heavy cream
1½ tablespoons fresh mint leaves
1 teaspoon caraway seeds

Serves 6
Preparation time: **10 minutes**
Cooking time: **about 5 minutes**

Put the white chocolate in a bowl, stand it in a *bain-marie*, and melt it gently over low heat, stirring with a wooden spoon until smooth. In a saucepan, bring the milk and cream to a boil. As soon as it begins to bubble, toss in the mint leaves and caraway seeds, remove from the heat, and cover the pan. Leave to infuse for 10 minutes, then strain the milk mixture through a wire-mesh conical sieve onto the melted chocolate. Mix with a whisk until thoroughly amalgamated.

Transfer the sauce to a clean saucepan, set over medium heat, and bubble for a few seconds, whisking continuously. Serve the sauce hot. If you are not serving it immediately, you can keep it warm in a *bain-marie* for a few minutes.

Walnut Ice Cream

If possible, use fresh "wet" walnuts for this recipe so that the ice cream retains a pale creamy color and looks almost like vanilla ice cream. The walnut flavor will come as a delicious surprise. If you use unshelled walnuts, allow an extra 20–30 minutes' preparation time. You will need 1 pound walnuts in the shell.

Serves 6
Preparation time: **15 minutes**
Churning time: **about 20 minutes**

Ingredients:
1 recipe Crème Anglaise (page 33), made without vanilla
2 cups shelled fresh walnuts, peeled
1 teaspoon sugar

Put aside 6 large walnut pieces for decoration and break up the rest into small pieces. Make the *crème anglaise*, adding the broken walnuts to the boiling milk just before mixing it into the egg yolks.

When the custard is ready, put it into a bowl and let cool. Pour it into a food processor or blender (1) and whizz for 2–3 minutes until smooth, then churn for about 20 minutes in an ice-cream maker (2 and 3).

If you prefer a really smooth texture, remove the walnuts from the custard just before churning the ice cream. I prefer to leave them in for a fuller flavor; the texture will be slightly grainy, but still soft.

To make the decoration, sprinkle the sugar into a nonstick skillet and cook until melted. Add the reserved walnuts and roll them in the sugar with a fork (4). Lift out each walnut separately and put on a baking sheet lined with parchment paper. Leave until cold. Decorate each scoop of ice cream with a sugar-coated walnut.

Honey Ice Cream

For an unusual treat, put a spoonful of ice cream in a chilled coffee cup and pour over some very hot coffee. Do this at the table so that you can immediately enjoy the delectable contrast of the piping hot coffee with the very cold ice cream.

Ingredients:

1 recipe Crème Anglaise (page 33), made with only ⅓ cup sugar
½ cup honey
½ cup heavy cream

Serves 6
Preparation time: **15 minutes**
Churning time: **about 30 minutes**

To make the *crème anglaise*, follow the recipe on page 33 adding the honey to the milk before boiling. You will only need ⅓ cup sugar, as the honey is so sweet. Leave the custard in a cool place until completely cold.

Pass the cold custard through a conical sieve directly into an ice cream maker and churn for about 10 minutes, until still fairly soft. Add the cream and churn for 10–20 minutes longer, until firm. Serve at once, or freeze for only a short time.

Saffron Ice Cream

This lovely ice cream has a heavenly color and a glorious flavor. It tastes even better if you make the custard 24 hours before churning. Serve the ice cream in meringue nests.

Ingredients:

1 recipe Crème Anglaise (page 33), made without vanilla
A pinch of saffron threads
½ cup heavy cream

Serves 8
Preparation time: **15 minutes**
Churning time: **10–20 minutes**

Make the *crème anglaise* and pass it through a conical sieve. Immediately add the saffron threads and let cool, stirring from time to time.

Pour the cooled custard into an ice cream maker and churn for 10–20 minutes, adding the cream some 5–8 minutes before the end of the process. When the ice cream is half-frozen, scrape off any saffron threads sticking to the paddle and mix them into the ice cream. Serve as soon as possible.

Serve Honey Ice Cream in a coffee cup with hot coffee poured over

Cinnamon Ice Cream

This ice cream is delicious served on its own or with a spoonful of Rich Chocolate Sauce (page 50). It also tastes divine served on a delicate, warm apple tart.

Ingredients:
1 recipe Crème Anglaise (page 33), made without vanilla
8 cinnamon sticks
½ cup heavy cream

Serves 6
Preparation time: **15 minutes**
Churning time: **about 30 minutes**

Make the *crème anglaise,* substituting the cinnamon sticks for the vanilla. Leave them in the custard while it is cooling.

When the custard is cold, pass it through a conical sieve directly into an ice cream maker, discarding the cinnamon sticks. Churn for about 10 minutes; the ice cream should still be fairly soft. Add the heavy cream and churn for another 20 minutes or so, until firm. Serve immediately, or freeze for only a short time.

Banana Ice Cream

Make sure that you use very ripe bananas to produce the correct flavor when making this ice cream. Serve it in small dishes, topped with marrons glacés*, or with a hot chocolate sauce (pages 50–51) for an indulgent treat.*

Ingredients:
1 recipe Crème Anglaise (page 33), made with 8 egg yolks
⅔ cup heavy cream
3 large very ripe bananas
4 tablespoons white rum

Makes 2 quarts
Preparation time: **15 minutes**
Churning time: **About 25 minutes**

When the *crème anglaise* is completely cold, stir in the cream. Put the peeled bananas in a food processor or blender with the rum and blend until smooth. Stir into the custard and put half the mixture at a time into an ice cream maker. Churn for about 25 minutes, until almost firm. Repeat with the remaining mixture. Pack the ice cream into storage containers as soon as it is ready; then store it in the freezer until you are ready to use it. Allow about 30 minutes in the refrigerator before serving.

Mint Chocolate Ice Cream

Serve this wonderful ice cream with a hot Chocolate Sauce (pages 50–51) for an indulgent treat.

Ingredients:

1 quart milk

1½ cups fresh mint, rinsed, dried, and minced

1¼ cups sugar

6 ounces bittersweet chocolate

¾ cup unsweetened cocoa powder, sifted

8 egg yolks

4 tablespoons mint liqueur (optional)

⅔ cup heavy cream

Makes 6–7 cups

Preparation time: **15 minutes**

Churning time: **About 25 minutes**

Because of the chocolate in this recipe, the custard will seem to have reached the right texture after being poured onto the egg yolks, but it will still be necessary to poach the mixture to make sure it is cooked.

To prepare the custard, first bring the milk, the mint, and ⅓ cup sugar to a boil. Meanwhile, put the chocolate, broken in sections, and the sifted cocoa powder, in a bowl. In a separate bowl, whisk the egg yolks and the rest of the sugar. When the milk boils, pour it onto the chocolate and cocoa powder, stirring quickly. When the chocolate has melted, pour it onto the egg yolks and sugar, again stirring continuously. Pour the liquid back into the pan and set it over low heat, still stirring, until the custard is thick enough to coat the back of the spoon. On no account let the custard boil. Chill in the refrigerator for 24 hours to let the flavors develop.

Strain and stir in the liqueur, if using, and the cream. Put half the mixture in the ice cream maker to churn for about 25 minutes, until fairly firm. Repeat with the remaining mixture.

As soon as the ice cream is ready, pack it into storage containers, then store it in the freezer. Allow about 30 minutes in the refrigerator before serving.

Passion-Fruit and Orange Sorbet

Everyone loves this refreshing, revitalizing sorbet, with its delightful vibrant color. I serve it in the passion-fruit shell like a boiled egg, with a few passion-fruit seeds scattered on top of the sorbet.

Ingredients:
1 cup passion-fruit pulp
Scant 1 cup orange juice
Juice of ½ lemon
Scant 1 cup Stock Syrup (page 10)

Serves 8
Preparation time: **10 minutes**
Churning time: **10–20 minutes**

Put all the ingredients in a blender and whizz for 3 minutes, then strain the purée through a conical sieve. Keep the liquid in the refrigerator until ready to churn. Churn in an ice cream maker for 10–20 minutes, until the sorbet is perfectly smooth and velvety. It tastes best when freshly churned, but can be kept in the freezer for several days.

Raspberry Sorbet

With their delicious flavor and texture, raspberries make a perfect sorbet. You can use thawed frozen raspberries instead of fresh—it will make little difference.

Ingredients:
1 pound raspberries, rinsed briefly, and thoroughly dried
Juice of ½ lemon
1 cup Stock Syrup (page 10)

Serves 6
Preparation time: **10 minutes**
Churning time: **10–20 minutes**

Put the raspberries in a food processor or blender and blend until smooth. Rub the purée through a nylon sieve set over a bowl, then strain in the lemon juice. Stir in the syrup, cover, and chill in the refrigerator. When the mixture is thoroughly chilled, transfer it to the ice cream maker and churn for about 8 minutes, until firm.

Pack into storage containers and store in the freezer until ready to serve. Take the sorbet out of the freezer and place in the refrigerator 20 minutes before serving.

Passion-Fruit and Orange Sorbet served in a passion-fruit shell

Apple Sorbet

This sorbet looks particularly effective if it is served in an apple shell. Simply scoop out the flesh from two apples and fill with the sorbet just before serving.

Ingredients:

8 ounces green apples (e.g. Granny Smith)
1 cup water
½ cup sugar
Juice of 1 lemon
2 tablespoons Calvados (optional)

Serves 4–6

Preparation time: **10 minutes**

Cooking time: **About 20 minutes, plus 15–20 minutes churning**

Wash the apples in cold water, cut in four, and remove the cores. Place in a saucepan with the water, sugar, and lemon juice. Poach gently for about 20 minutes, until tender. Put the apple segments with the poaching liquid in a blender, purée for 3 minutes, then pass through a conical sieve. Let the purée cool at room temperature. Once it is cold, cover with plastic wrap and keep in the refrigerator until you are ready to churn.

Immediately before serving, add the Calvados, if using, then churn the apple purée in an ice cream maker for 15–20 minutes.

Pack into storage containers and freeze until ready to serve. Allow about 30 minutes in the refrigerator before serving.

Rose-Petal Sorbet

Roses give this ravishingly pretty dessert a delicate, scented flavor, full of romance. In summer, you could use roses from your own garden to make this delicious sorbet. Try to use purplish-red roses, plus one of another color.

Ingredients:

Petals from 24 medium-size, scented roses, total weight about 4 ounces

2¼ cups sugar

1¼ cups water

Juice of 1 lemon

Serves 4–6

Preparation time: **15 minutes, plus 3–4 hours drying the petals**

Churning time: **20–25 minutes**

Wash the rose petals gently in very cold water. Put the sugar in a small saucepan with half the water, dissolve over low heat, then boil for 2 minutes and skim. Take the pan off the heat and drop in about ten of the most attractive petals, including a few of a different color from the red (yellow, for instance). Leave the petals in the syrup until cold, then lift them out one by one, shake off the excess syrup, and spread them out well apart on a wire rack. Reserve the syrup in the pan. Let the petals drain for 3–4 hours.

Add the remining water to the rose syrup, then add the lemon juice. Bring to a boil and drop in all the, by now, lightly crystallized rose petals. Take the pan off the heat, let cool at room temperature, then refrigerate for 1–2 hours.

Strain the rose-petal syrup through a conical sieve, pour into an ice cream maker and churn for 20–25 minutes. The texture of the sorbet should be soft and creamy, and the color divinely pink.

Serve the sorbet as soon as it is ready. If you churn it too long before serving, it will lose its lightness. Scoop it into glass coupes or bowls and arrange the crystallized rose petals around the edge and on top.

Tea, Mint, and Prune Sorbet

This combination of Darjeeling tea, fresh mint and prunes may sound unusual but it is simple to make and produces a very successful sorbet.

Ingredients:
¾ cup plus 2 tablespoons sugar
4 cups water
⅔ cup Darjeeling tea leaves
1 ounce mint, rinsed and dried
1¼ cups pitted prunes

Makes 5 cups
Preparation time: *5 minutes, plus 12 hours infusing*
Churning time: *10–20 minutes*

Combine the sugar and water in a saucepan and bring to a boil. Have the tea leaves and mint ready in one bowl, the prunes in another. Pour the boiling syrup over the tea and mint, cover, and leave to infuse for 3 minutes. Strain immediately into the bowl containing the prunes. Cool, cover, and leave overnight in the refrigerator.

The following day, pour the liquid into the ice cream maker (you will probably need to do 2 batches), reserving the prunes. Churn for 18–20 minutes.

Meanwhile, slice the prunes lengthwise into 6. Add these in the last minute of churning, when the sorbet is formed.

Serve at once. You can store this sorbet in the freezer for a brief time, but it is not advisable to leave it there for more than 2 hours. It will need a good 30 minutes in the refrigerator before serving. In the freezer, the little pieces of prune become frozen hard, and time is needed in the refrigerator to ensure an even texture throughout the sorbet before it is eaten. Otherwise your guests might break their teeth on frozen prunes!

Index

A

almonds: frangipane, 48
apples: apple sorbet, 60
   autumnal sauce, 29
apricots: hot apricot sauce, 22
armagnac: grape coulis with armagnac, 16
   prune and armagnac sauce, 30
autumnal sauce, 29

B

bananas: autumnal sauce, 29
   banana ice cream, 56
   banana sauce, 29
   honey sauce, 24
blackberry coulis, 12
black-currant coulis, 11
butter, 6
   buttercream, 45
   chocolate cream, 49
   frangipane, 48
   hot caramel butter sauce, 22
   mousseline cream, 48
   orange butter sauce, 31

C

calvados: apple sorbet, 60
caramel: caramel sabayon, 39
   caramel sauce, 26
   hot caramel butter sauce, 22
   praline cream, 46
   rich caramel sauce, 27
cardamom: autumnal sauce, 29
Chantilly cream, 45
   chocolate Chantilly cream, 45
   coffee Chantilly cream, 45
   praline cream, 46
Chiboust cream, 42
   chocolate Chiboust cream, 42
chocolate, 6
   chocolate Chantilly cream, 45
   chocolate Chiboust cream, 42
   chocolate cream, 49
   chocolate crème anglaise, 33
   light chocolate sauce, 50
   mint chocolate ice cream, 57
   quick chocolate sauce, 51
   rich chocolate sauce, 50
   white chocolate sauce with mint, 51
cinnamon ice cream, 56
coffee: coffee Chantilly cream, 45
   coffee crème anglaise, 33
   coffee sabayon with Tia Maria, 38
coulis, 7, 9, 10-21
   blackberry, 12
   black-currant, 11
   grape with armagnac, 16
   grapefruit with mint, 10
   mango with saffron, 18
   peaches with scented honey, 19
   pears with red wine, 14
   red fruit, 15
   red-currant, 11
   rhubarb, 15
   strawberry with green peppercorns, 12
   white peach with star anise, 20
creams, 7
   buttercream, 45
   Chantilly cream, 45
   Chiboust cream, 42
   chocolate cream, 49
   frangipane, 48
   mousseline cream, 48
   pastry cream, 41
   praline cream, 46
crème anglaise, 9, 33
   banana ice cream, 56
   chocolate crème anglaise, 33
   cinnamon ice cream, 56
   coffee crème anglaise, 33
   honey ice cream, 55
   saffron ice cream, 55
   walnut ice cream, 52
crème fraîche: banana sauce, 29
custard sauces: crème anglaise, 33

D

Darjeeling tea: tea, mint, and prune sorbet, 62

E

eggs, 6
   caramel sabayon, 39
   coffee sabayon with Tia Maria, 38
   crème anglaise, 33
   Italian meringue, 44
   jasmine tea sauce, 35
   kirsch sabayon, 36
   lemon sauce, 34
   pastry cream, 41

F

flour, 6
frangipane, 48
fruit coulis see coulis

G

gelatin, 6
golden raisins: rum sauce, 24
grape coulis with armagnac, 16
grapefruit coulis with mint, 10
green peppercorns, strawberry coulis with, 12

H

hazelnuts: praline cream, 46
honey: autumnal sauce, 29
   coulis of peaches with scented honey, 19
   honey ice cream, 55
   honey sauce, 24
hot caramel butter sauce, 22

I

ice creams, 7
   banana, 56
   cinnamon, 56
   honey, 55
   mint chocolate, 57
   saffron, 55
   walnut, 52
Italian meringue, 44
   buttercream, 45
   Chiboust cream, 42

J

jasmine tea sauce, 35

K

kirsch sabayon, 36

L

lemon sauce, 34
light chocolate sauce, 50
licorice sauce, 26

M

mango coulis with saffron, 18
meringue: buttercream, 45
   Chiboust cream, 42
   Italian meringue, 44
mint: grapefruit coulis with mint, 10
   mint chocolate ice cream, 57

Index

mint sauce, 23
tea, mint, and prune sorbet, 62
white chocolate sauce with mint, 51
mousseline cream, 48

O
oranges: orange butter sauce, 31
passion-fruit and orange sorbet, 58
red wine sauce, 25

P
passion-fruit and orange sorbet, 58
pastry cream, 41
mousseline cream, 48
praline cream, 46
peaches: coulis of peaches with scented honey, 19
white peach coulis with star anise, 20
pears: coulis of pears with red wine, 14
peppercorns: strawberry coulis with green peppercorns, 12
praline cream, 46
prunes: prune and armagnac sauce, 30
tea, mint, and prune sorbet, 62

Q
quick chocolate sauce, 51

R
raspberries: raspberry sorbet, 58
red-fruit coulis, 15
red-wine sauce, 25
red-currant coulis, 11
rhubarb coulis, 15
rich caramel sauce, 27
rich chocolate sauce, 50
rose-petal sorbet, 61
rum: banana sauce, 29
frangipane, 48
rum sauce, 24

S
sabayons: caramel, 39
coffee with Tia Maria, 38
kirsch, 36
saffron: mango coulis with saffron, 18
saffron ice cream, 55
sorbets, 7
apple, 60
passion-fruit and orange, 58
raspberry, 58
rose-petal, 61
tea, mint, and prune, 62
scented honey, coulis of peaches with, 19
star anise, white peach coulis with, 20
stock syrup, 10
strawberries: red-fruit coulis, 15
strawberry coulis with green peppercorns, 12
sugar, 6
syrup, sorbet or stock, 10

T
tea: jasmine tea sauce, 35
tea, mint, and prune sorbet, 62
Tia Maria, coffee sabayon with, 38

W
walnut ice cream, 52
white chocolate sauce with mint, 51
white peach coulis with star anise, 20
wine: coulis of pears with red wine, 14
red-wine sauce, 25

This edition published in 2005 by
Quadrille Publishing Ltd
Alhambra House
27–31 Charing Cross Road
London WC2H 0LS

Based on material originally published in *Sauces; sweet and savory, classic and new* by Michel Roux.

Text © 1996 & 2000 Michel Roux
Photography © 1996 & 2000 Martin Brigdale
Design & layout © 2000
Quadrille Publishing Ltd

Publishing Director: Anne Furniss
Art Director: Mary Evans
Art Editor: Rachel Gibson
Project Editor & Translator: Kate Whiteman
Editorial Assistant: Caroline Perkins
Styling: Helen Trent
Production: Rachel Wells

All rights reserved. No part of this book may be reproduced, stored in a retrieval system or transmitted in any form or by any means, electronic, electrostatic, magnetic tape, mechanical, photocopying, recording or otherwise, without the permission in writing of the publisher.

The right of Michel Roux to be identified as the Author of this Work has been asserted by him in accordance with the Copyright, Designs and Patents Act 1988.

Cataloguing-in-Publication Data: a catalogue record for this book is available from the British Library.

ISBN 1 84400 188 1

Printed in China through World Print Ltd.